Aadab-e-biryani

INDIAN
Biryanis Recipes

Published 2008 by
Prakash Books India Pvt. Ltd.
1, Ansari Road, Daryaganj
New Delhi 110 002, India.
E-mail: sales@prakashbooks.com
Website: www.prakashbooks.com
Tel: 011-23247062-65

© 2008 Prakash Books India Pvt. Ltd.

© Rasoi is a property of STAR India Pvt. Ltd.

ISBN: 978-81-7234-250-0

Printed & bound in India at: Presstech Litho Pvt. Ltd.

Aadab-e-biryani

INDIAN
Biryanis Recipes

STAR
Rasoi

Inspired by STAR TV Shows

Contents

Introduction

The origin of the Biryani, and its appearance in India, is shrouded in mystery and legend. Its name is from a Farsi word, but it is not clear if the dish itself is Persian in origin. Whether it came with Arab traders along India's west coast or with the armies of Timur from Kazakstan, its popularity and refinement in India certainly happened under the Moghuls. In Delhi's imperial kitchen, supervised by Unani physicians, the Biryani comes into written history in the recipe books, where it is listed under Lashkar-e-khana, or food for soldiers. Whether it was with Timur or his grandson Babar, the Biryani accompanied the armies from Uzbekistan, cooking slowly for the whole day in single sealed pots, while the cavalry either scouted or battled on the craggy Afghan ridges or along the vast plains of the Indus Valley. Obviously, it was eaten leisurely at sunset.

Looking at the Biryani served in modern-day Uzbekistan – cooked in sheep's fat and served without any spices except dried chillies – it is sure that the Mughals learnt the glories of clarified butter, or ghee, and the aroma of the 21 legendary spices only when they came to India. This must be the contribution of Hindu cooks or helpers who were employed locally when the Mughal Empire had settled down to rule India. Akbar's marriage to the Rajput princess Jodha Bai certainly contributed to further infiltrations into the imperial kitchen. Like the Mughals themselves, the Biryani traveled to other parts of India and local culinary skills and tastes must have contributed further to present differences in its regional character.

The most sophisticated, of course, is the Avadhi Biryani that evolved from the seat of power in Lucknow. Refinements like putting spices into small bags of muslin – so that they don't get to your teeth – must have come from Avadhi cooking itself. The Avadhi Biryani traveled to Calcutta when Nawab Wajid Ali Shah was deposed after the Sepoy Mutiny, and brought to the imperial capital. Today, the Calcutta Biryani is one of a kind, with its addition of boiled eggs and potatoes. Incidentally, the potato came as an indicator of whether the rice and meat had cooked properly once the sealed pot was opened.

History has several contributions to the Biryani like other items of Mughlai food. The Hindu presence in the royal kitchen led to the creation of vegetarian Mughlai food – an incomprehensible idea before Jodha Bai's appearance. The discovery of the Tahiri Biryani, which uses no meat at all, opens up the glory of vegetables cooked in rice, anointed with ghee and spices. Another form of the Biryani that has a considerably large constituency in southern India is the Hyderabadi version, which is accompanied by a sour and chilly-hot curry, and yogurt salad called a raita, which may look innocent but may cause frenzy among those not familiar with the Andhra palate. The Bombay Biryani is a variation on the same theme. The Gujarati Bohra Biriyan – apart from the spelling and the pronunciation – has a character quite its own, particularly for those who enjoy a hint of sweet.

Pakistan is known to offer a mind-boggling variety in Biryanis, each subtly different from each other. But the overwhelming popularity has been reserved for the Sindhi version, which is a revelation in terms of taste and aroma. In Bangladesh, the Biryani has found its own interpretations, though the most exciting one among them uses fish, in fact, the ever-popular hilsa. Trust the Bengalis to bring their fish wherever they can, with infallible effect. Burmese Muslims have a version of the Biryani they call a danpauk, which is also distinctive.

Usually, the Biryani is a complete meal, cooked in a single pot, but further regional refinements have included accompaniments like a korma, or curry. Personal taste or interest can always add and subtract these accompanants, but one cannot deny the variety they offer.

Egg Plant Biryani

Ingredients:

Brinjal (cut into ½" cubes)	: 400 gms	Mustard seeds	: 1½ tsp
Brown rice (washed, soaked in water for 30 mins and drained)	: 2 cups	Garam masala powder	: 1 tsp
		Coriander powder	: ½ tsp
Water	: 4 cups	Cayenne powder	: 1 pinch
Turmeric	: 2½ tsp	Black pepper powder	: 1 pinch
Butter	: 4 tbsp	Red bell pepper (sliced)	: 1
Poppy seeds	: 1 tsp	Onion (sliced)	: 1
		Garlic (crushed)	: 2 cloves

Procedure:

1) Take a heavy bottomed saucepan. Put in 1 tsp salt, 2 tsp turmeric powder, water and rice into it. Wait till it boils and then cover it and simmer till rice is done.

2) Now, take another large saucepan. Put the butter into it and heat it.

3) Next, put the poppy and mustard seeds. Stir for 2 minutes before you add the remaining turmeric, garam masala, coriander, cayenne, and black pepper powders. Cook it for 2 minutes, stirring it all the while.

4) Then add the onion, red pepper and the egg plant. This will have to be cooked till the vegetables become tender. This will take around 10 minutes. To this add the garlic and continue to cook for 2 minutes.

5) As the last and the most important step, mix the rice and the vegetables together.

Vegetarian Biryani

Serves: 6–8

Cooking time (approx.): 60 minutes

Ingredients:

Basmati rice (washed and soaked in water for 30 mins) : 400 gms
Cauliflowers (cut into florets) : 250 gms
Green peas (shelled) : 100 gms
Carrot (sliced into 2.5 cm long pieces) : 100 gms
French beans (sliced into diamond shaped pieces) : 100 gms
Potato (each cut into four pieces) : 3
Black cardamoms : 2
Green cardamoms : 4
Cinnamon : 4 cm
Cloves : 4
Peppercorns : 8
Shahjeera : 1 tsp
Bay leaves : 3
Saffron : A few strands

Water as required

For the extra spice:

Onions (sliced) : 250 gms
Curd : ¾ cup
Chilli powder : 4 tsp
Ginger-Garlic paste : 3 tsp
Mint paste : 2 tsp
Garam masala powder : 1½ tsp
Coriander-Cumin powder : 1½ tsp
Ghee : 3 tsp or more

Ghee for deep frying onions
Salt as per taste

For garnishing:

Tomatoes (sliced) : 2
Capsicum (sliced) : 2
Onions (that have been fried till they become crisp) : 2
Mint leaves : A few

Procedure:

For the vegetables:

1) Wash the vegetables well and dry them thoroughly.
2) Mix all the other spices except the onions and marinate the vegetables in it for an hour.

3) *Now, when the vegetables marinate in the spices, fry the onions in ghee till they are brown. Once done, remove it from the ghee. When it is cool, grind it into a paste.*

4) *Cook the rice in double the amount of water. When it is cooked, spread it in a plate and wait till it is cool.*

For the rice:

1) *First roast the saffron mildly, grind it into a powder and then spread it over the rice.*

2) *Next, take a kadhai, put the ghee in it and heat. Also, season it with the whole spices. To this add the vegetables and saute for say, 5 minutes.*

3) *Then add 1 cup water and cook the vegetables, onion paste till they are done and become almost dry.*

4) *Next, take a baking dish. Place the rice and the vegetables in alternate layers in the baking dish. Just to make sure that your biryani doesn't only look good but tastes good as well, garnish the top layer and then bake it in a moderately hot oven for 20 minutes.*

To serve: *Serve hot with papad and raita.*

Kofta Biryani

Serves: 2–3

Cooking time (approx.): 60 minutes

Ingredients:

Basmati rice (washed, soaked in water for 30 mins and drained)	: 1 cup	Lemon juice	: 1 tsp
		Bay leaf	: 1
		Tomato puree	: ½ cup
Chick peas (Chana) (cooked and mashed)	: 1 cup	Palak (spinach) puree	: ½ cup
Ginger	: 2" pieces	Turmeric	: A pinch
Garlic	: 2 cloves	Cream (optional)	: 2 tbsp
Onion	: 1 cup	Chilli powder	: ½ tsp
Green chillies	: 3–4	Oil/ghee as required	
		Salt as per taste	

Procedure:

1) Put the oil or ghee in a pan, heat it and then put the bay leaf.

2) Next, add the grained basmati rice and fry it till the fragrance comes out. Then add 2 cups of water, a little salt and cook the rice. However, it should be kept in mind that the grains should remain separated even after cooking.

3) Make a paste of garlic, ½ cup onion, green chillies, lemon juice and ginger (1"). Add this to the chana, mix well, make small balls out of them and deep fry in oil.

4) Next, put oil or ghee in another pan and heat it. Put the remaining grated ginger and finely chopped onion. Continue to fry it till the onions turn light brown.

5) Now, add the palak puree, tomato puree, chilli powder, turmeric, cream and salt. Mix everything well and cook it for 5 to 10 minutes or till the gravy becomes thick.

6) Take a serving bowl, then spread a layer of rice, followed by a layer of gravy, which in turn is followed by a layer of kofta. This order should be maintained till all the rice, gravy and kofta is finished. Care should be taken to see that the top layer is of rice.

Tips:
*   Remember to arrange the layers only a few minutes before serving, else the koftas soften and lose their taste. Plus, care should also be taken to see that the koftas do not break while serving.

Kabuli Chana Biryani

Serves: 4
Cooking time (approx.): 60 minutes

Ingredients:

Coriander leaves (chopped): 3 tbsp	Garlic paste : 1 tsp
Mint leaves(chopped) : 2 tbsp	Red chilli powder : 1 tsp
Green chillies (chopped) : ½ tsp	Turmeric powder (haldi) : ½ tsp
Saffron (dissolved in ¼ cup	Fresh low fat curd (dahi) : 1 cup
warm low fat milk) : ¼ tsp	Tomatoes (chopped) : ¾ cup
Oil (for greasing) : 1 tsp	Potatoes (peeled and cubed) : 1 cup
Water : 3 cups	Green chillies (finely
	chopped) : 1½ tsp
For the kabuli chana gravy:	Oil : 1 tbsp
Kabuli chana (chick peas) : ½ cup	Salt to taste
Ginger paste : 1 tsp	

Procedure:

1) Soak kabuli chana overnight in a little water and boil in a pressure cooker till tender.
2) Heat a little oil in a non-stick pan.
3) Add to this the ginger and garlic pastes and fry for a while.
4) Next, add the red chilli powder, turmeric powder, 2 teaspoons of water and fry for a minute. Then add the curd, tomatoes, potatoes and green chillies and stir them all for a moment.
5) Now, add the cooked kabuli chana to it, mix them well and set the mixture aside.
6) Next, add coriander, mint leaves, green chillies and saffron milk to the cooked rice.

7) Once mixed, keep it aside. Now make 5 layers on a greased baking dish. The five layers are: 1/3 of the rice, ½ the kabuli chana gravy, 1/3 of the rice, rest of the chana gravy, and the last layer of rice.

8) Cover with an aluminium foil and then bake it for 20 mins in a pre-heated oven at 200°C or 375°F.

To serve: Serve hot.

Soya Biryani

Serves: 4

Cooking time (approx.): 60 minutes

Ingredients:

To prepare the rice:

Soyabeans (soaked overnight)	: ½ cup
Long grained rice (cooked)	: 1 cup
Cinnamon	: 1 stick
Cardamom	: 1
Bay leaf	: 1
Salt as per taste	

To prepare the masala mixture:

Onions (sliced)	: ½ cup
Cumin seeds	: ½ tsp
Ginger-Garlic paste	: 1 tsp
Tomatoes (chopped)	:1 cup
Turmeric powder	: ½ tsp
Chilli powder	: ½ tsp
Coriander powder	: ½ tsp
Fresh thick curd	: ¼ cup
Mixed boiled vegetables (peas, french beans, cauliflower, etc.)	: 1½ cup
Mint leaves (chopped)	: ¼ cup
Coriander leaves (chopped)	: ¼ cup
Ghee	: 1tbsp
Salt as per taste	

Procedure:

For the rice:

1) Wash the soya beans and drain the water.

2) To this add 2 cups of water, cinnamon, cardamom, bay leaf and salt and cook all the ingredients over a medium flame. When done, drain the excess water.

3) Now, mix the cooked rice and the soyabeans and keep aside.

For the masala mixture:

1) First, heat the oil in a non-stick pan. Add the cumin seeds to it and wait till they crackle.

2) Then add the onions and the ginger-garlic paste and saute. Cook till the onions turn brown.

3) Next, put the tomatoes, coriander powder, chilli powder, turmeric powder and ¼ cup of water. Cook till the water dries up, leaving behind the tomatoes soft.

4) To this, add the curd, salt and the boiled vegetables. Mix everything well. Simmer for 5 to 7 minutes till it is semi-dry.

5) Finally add the coriander and the mint leaves.

6) Now, arrange the preparation in layers — spread half of the soyabean and rice on a baking dish (200 mm/ 8″ diameter). On this layer, spread the entire masala mixture. Then as the last layer, spread the rest of the rice and soya bean. Cover it with aluminum foil.

7) Bake for 20 to 30 minutes in a pre-heated oven (180 °C/ 360 °F).

To serve: Serve hot.

Mushroom Biryani

Serves: 8

Cooking time (approx.): 30 minutes

Ingredients:

Mushroom	: 1 kg	Cardamoms	: 3
Onions	: 2	Cloves	: 3
Basmati rice	: 4 cups	Tomatoes	: 3
Lemon juice	: 1	Chilli powder	: 1½ tsp
Oil and ghee	: ¾ cups	Coriander powder	: 3 tsp
Soya sauce	: 2 tsp	Mint leaves	: A few
Garlic	: 7 cloves	Coriander leaves	: A few
Green chillies	: 4	Water	: 7 cups
Ginger (chopped)	: 3 tsp	Salt to taste	
Cinnamon	: 3 sticks		

Procedure:

1) Soak the rice in water for an hour.

2) Trim the mushrooms into big pieces. Also, cut the chillies, onions and tomatoes.

3) Make a paste by grinding cardamom, cloves, ginger, cinnamon and garlic.

4) Put some oil and ghee in a pressure cooker. Fry ground masala and onions till the latter turn golden brown. Next, add the mushrooms and all the other ingredients to it and stir for 10 mins.

5) Next, add 7 cups of water to it and let it boil. Take the soaked rice and add it to the mixture. Stir till the levels of both the rice and the water becomes equal.

6) Cook it in a pressure cooker over a low flame for 15 mins.

Navratna Biryani

Ingredients:

Basmati rice	: 2½ cups	Cinnamon	: 1 stick
Green colour (dissolved in 1 tsp water)	: 6 drops	Cloves	: 6
		Peppercorns	: 12
Red colour (dissolved in 1 tsp water)	: 4 drops	Green cardamoms	: 4
		Ginger (minced)	: 2" piece
Peas (boiled)	: 60 gms	Garlic (minced)	: 6 cloves
Egg white (boiled and chopped)	: 60 gms	Onions (sliced)	: 60 gms
		Ghee	: 60 gms
Tomatoes (diced)	: 60 gms	Water	: 4½ cups
Cumin seeds	: ½ tsp	Nuts for garnishing (almonds, cashews and sultanas)	
Green chillies (finely chopped)	: 2	Salt as per taste	
Coriander leaves	: 1 tsp		

Procedure:

1) Wash the rice properly and then soak in water.
2) Put ghee in a pan and heat. Then put in the garlic and onion and fry.
3) When done, add the whole spices, ginger, salt, green chillies, cumin seeds and saute.
4) Now, take the rice along with the water and add it to the pan. Cook till tender.
5) When the rice is done, divide it into three parts. Add green colour, coriander leaves and peas to the first part and mix well.
6) Add the diced tomatoes and the red color to the second part and mix well too.
7) Now in the third part, add the chopped egg white.
8) Arrange the three portions as three different layers.
9) Garnish it with almonds, cashew nuts and sultanas.

Chicken Dum Biryani

Serves: 4

Cooking time (approx.): 40 minutes

Ingredients:

Chicken	: 800 gms	Green chillies	: 6
Yoghurt	: 1 cup	Coriander and Mint leaves	
Red chilli powder	: 1 tsp	(chopped and mixed)	: 1 cup
Turmeric powder	: 1 tsp	Poppy seeds	: 8 tbsp
Garam masala powder	: 1 tsp	Tomatoes (medium	
Basmati rice	: 2 cups	sized and chopped)	: 2
Milk	: 1 tbsp	Onions (medium sized	
Water	: 6 cups	and chopped)	: 2
Cinnamon (broken)	: 2" sticks	Ghee/Butter	: 4 tbsp
Bay leaves	: 4	Saffron (dissolved	
Cloves	: 4	in some warm milk)	: 2 tsp
Black cardamoms	: 4	Potatoes (medium sized, boiled,	
Green cardamoms	: 4	halved and deep fried)	: 6
Black peppercorns	: 1 tsp	Onions (large sized,	
Cumin seeds	: 1 tsp	cut into rings)	: 2
Ginger (chopped)	: 1 tbsp	Cashew nuts and raisins (for	
Garlic (chopped)	: 1 tbsp	garnishing)	
Mace	: 1 blade	Sheet of aluminum foil for sealing	
Nutmeg (grated)	: 1 tsp	Salt as per taste	

Procedure:

1) Put a little clarified butter/ghee in a pan, heat it and fry onion rings in it till they turn brown.

2) Make a paste by grinding a small portion of the browned onions, ginger, garlic, mace, nutmeg, green chillies, coriander-mint leaves, poppy seeds, tomatoes, chopped

onions and half of the cinnamon, cloves, black-green cardamoms, black peppercorns and bay leaves.

3) Next, take the chicken pieces and make some cuts on them.

4) Take a bowl and put in it the yoghurt, red chilli powder, garam masala powder, turmeric powder and the ground paste with some salt. Mix well and rub this mixture on the chicken pieces. The paste needs to enter the chicken pieces. So leave it for at least an hour.

5) Combine the rice, water, milk, remaining whole spices (except cumin seeds) and salt in a large vessel. Cook this till the rice is half-done. When that's done, drain away the excess liquid and then spread the rice on a plate to cool.

6) Put the clarified butter/ghee in a heavy-bottomed pan, heat it and when it is hot, splutter some cumin seeds. Then add the chicken pieces with the marinade and cook on a high flame. Do this for a few seconds. Now, take the fried potato halves. Add them to the chicken pieces and mix well. Cover it and cook on a low flame for 15 mins, or cook till the chicken is almost done. Remove from flame and keep aside.

7) Next, arrange the rice and the chicken in layers. To begin with, put the ghee/butter in the same heavy-bottomed vessel and arrange a layer of chicken with gravy, a layer of rice topped with a portion of brown onions and saffron milk. Repeat the same process, till all is used up. Keep the topmost layer of rice with melted clarified butter (ghee)/butter, browned onions and saffron milk on top of it.

8) Once the arrangement of the ingredients in layers is concluded, spread an aluminum foil on top of the pan and use a tight fitting lid to cover it.

9) Cook over a very low flame for the next 12 mins, placing the biryani on a tawa.

10) For garnishing, use fried cashew nuts and raisins.

To serve: Serve hot with Cucumber in Yoghurt (Kheere ka Raita)

Hyderabadi Chicken Biryani

Serves: 4
Cooking time (approx.): 40 minutes

Ingredients:

For the rice:

Basmati rice	: 2 cups
Water	: 3½ cups
Ghee	: 2–3 tsp
Cardamom	: 3
Cloves	: 3
Cinnamom	: 1" piece
Bay leaf	: 1
Shahjeera	: 1 tsp
Salt as per taste	

For the chicken:

Chicken	: 500 gms
Onions (finely sliced)	: 3
Tomatoes (finely chopped)	: 2
Coriander leaves (finely chopped)	: ½ bunch
Mint leaves (finely chopped)	: ½ bunch
Salt as per taste	

Whole garam masala for the chicken:

Cloves	: 3
Cinnamon	: 1" piece
Cardamom	: 3

Grind the following to a paste (paste 1)

Red chillies: 12
Fennel seeds: 2 tsp
Coriander seeds: 2 tbsp
Poppy seeds: 2 tsp
Garlic: 1 pod
Ginger: 2" piece

Grind the following to a paste (paste 2)

Coconut	: ½ cup
Curd	: ½ cup
Cashew nuts (chopped)	: 3 tsp
Raisins	: 3 tsp
Saffron: A pich	
Mitha Attar: 3–4 drops	

Procedure:

Cooking the rice:

1) Put ghee in a pan and heat it. Next, add bay leaf and the whole garam masala and fry for 30 seconds.

2) *Add rice and stir the mixture for a minute.*

3) *Next, add water and salt.*

4) *Cook on high heat till water starts boiling and then cover with lid and simmer till rice is done.*

Cooking the chicken:

1) *Heat oil in a pan. Put whole garam masala in it and fry.*

2) *Add to it the sliced onions and fry it till the onions turn brown.*

3) *Add to this Paste 1 and fry for 2 mins.*

4) *Next, add the tomatoes to this and fry it till the oil separates.*

5) *Now, add the chicken and mix it well. Also add the coriander and mint leaves.*

6) *Add salt and cook till done.*

7) *Now, add Paste 2 to this and cook for the next 2 mins.*

8) *Divide the cooked rice into 3 and the chicken into 2 parts.*

9) *Next, arrange the rice and the chicken in alternate layers. The bottom and the top layers should be that of rice.*

10) *Mix saffron in ¼ cup of warm milk and pour it over the arranged biryani along with mitha attar.*

11) *For garnishing, use raisins and cashew nuts.*

12) *Cover the pan with a lid and seal with an aluminum foil.*

13) *Cook it for 15–20 mins over a low flame, placing the vessel on a tawa.*

Kerala Style Chicken Biryani

Serves: 4–5

Cooking time (approx.): 75 minutes

Ingredients:

Basmati rice	: 2 cups	Yellow colour powder	: A pinch
Chicken	: 1½ kg	Onion (large sized)	: 3
Chilli powder	: ½ tsp	Tomato	: 3
Coriander powder	: 1½ tsp	Green chillies (slit)	: 2–3
Cinnamon	: 4 pieces	Oil for frying	
Cloves	: 6	Water	: 3½ cups
Cardamom	: 4	Salt as per taste	
Ginger (minced)	: 1" piece		
Garlic (minced)	: 8 pods	**Marinate with:**	
Mint leaves	: 2–3 stems	Chilli powder	: ½ tsp
Coriander leaves	: 2–3 stems	Coriander powder	: 1½ tsp
Cashews	: 20	Turmeric powder	: A pinch
Raisins	: 15	Black pepper powder	: A pinch
Ghee/Oil/Butter as required		Garlic-Ginger paste	: ½ tsp
Curd	: 3 tsp	Garam masala powder as per taste	
Rose essence	: 1 tsp	Lemon juice	: 5–6 drops

Procedure:

1) Put rice in water and let it soak for an hour. Then drain away the water and keep aside the rice.

2) Cut chicken into big pieces. Make slits on them.

3) Take all the ingredients mentioned above for marinating the chicken and mix them well.

4) Now, marinate the chicken in this mixture and leave for an hour. Alternately, you can prepare this the previous day and put it in a refrigerator.

5) Fry the chicken lightly adding salt, in oil.

6) Put 2–3 tsp of ghee in a thick-bottomed pan and heat it.

7) Add cinnamon, cloves and cardamom to the ghee and stir it for a few minutes.

8) Take the soaked and drained rice and add it to this ghee. Fry it for 10 mins.

9) Add water and 1 tsp of salt to it.

10) Cook it over a high flame and cover the pan with a lid.

11) After some time, when there is no more water visible on top of the rice, open the lid and stir the rice. Take care to ensure that the entire rice is mixed well. This is done to avoid burning the rice at the bottom of the vessel.

12) Once the entire water has evaporated, remove the rice from heat and cool.

13) Put a little ghee or oil or both in a pan or kadhai and heat it.

14) Add green chilli, garlic and ginger to this and saute.

15) Next, add onions and fry.

16) Add chilli powder, coriander powder and salt and saute once again.

17) Add curd and mix well.

18) Then add the chicken pieces along with the marinade.

19) Cover the mixture and cook for 10 mins.

20) Next, add big tomato slices and ½ tsp salt and cook covered till the gravy looks like a paste.

21) Fry raisins, cashews, coriander and mint leaves separately in ghee and keep them aside.

For baking biryani:

1. Oven Style:

1) In a greased flat dish, arrange the chicken (with gravy) and rice in layers. The first layer should be that of chicken and the topmost layer should be that of rice.

2) Mix rose essence and yellow colour powder and sprinkle it on top of the rice carefully.

3) Take one tsp of ghee and sprinkle it on top.

4) Sprinkle the fried leaves followed by fried cashews and raisins. Seal the vessel with aluminum foil.
5) Bake in an oven at 375°F or 185°C for the next 45 mins.

2. In the absence of oven:

1) Take a big wide vessel. Just coat it with butter or ghee.
2) Arrange the chicken and the cooked rice into layers as mentioned above.
3) Next, cover the vessel with a lid and heat it over a low flame for 20 to 25 mins placing it on a tawa.
4) The biryani is ready to be served.

To serve: Serve the biryani with raita made with curd, salt, onions, tomatoes and green chillies (optional).

Hyderabadi Dum Chicken Biryani

Serves: 10

Cooking time (approx.): **60 minutes**

Ingredients:

Chicken (cut into pieces)	: 1 whole	Coriander powder	: 3 tsp
Basmati rice (washed, soaked and drained for 30 mins)	: 5 cups	Cumin powder	: 1 tsp
		Cumin seeds	: ½ tsp
		Mint leaves	: ½ cup
Onions (medium sized, thinly sliced)	: 2	Chicken stock	: 7½ cups
		Saffron (soaked in 5 tbsp of lukewarm water)	: A few strands
Cardamom	: 5 pods		
Cinnamon	: 2 sticks	Onions (fried, for garnishing)	: 1
Cloves	: 6		
Garlic paste	: 1 tsp	Fresh coriander leaves (for garnishing)	: A bunch
Ginger paste	: 1 tsp		
Yoghurt	: 200 gms	Ghee/Cooking oil	: 200 gms
Turmeric powder	: ½ tsp	Salt as per taste	
Red chilli powder	: 1 tsp		

Procedure:

1) Mix the plain yogurt, turmeric powder, coriander powder, red chilli powder, ginger paste, garlic paste and cumin powder and marinate the chicken in this mixture for 1 hour.

2) Add sliced onions, mint and salt to the marinated chicken.

3) Put 50 gms ghee or oil, cinnamon sticks, cardamoms, cloves and cumin seeds to the boiling stock. Add rice and cook till it is cooked.

4) Now, add the rice to the chicken.

5) Next, pour the remaining ghee (or oil) and saffron water on the rice.
6) Cook the rice on dum for the next 30 to 45 mins or till it is fully cooked.
7) Garnish it with fried onion and chopped fresh coriander leaves and serve hot.

Chicken Biryani

Serves: 4–5

Cooking time (approx.): 35 minutes

Ingredients:

Basmati rice	: 2 cups	Cardamom powder	: ½ tsp
Chicken	: ¾ kg	Garam masala powder	: 2 tsp
Yoghurt	: 1 cup	Milk	: ½ cup
Onions (sliced)	: 3	Saffron	: A pinch
Ginger paste	: 1 tsp	Coriander powder	: 1 tsp
Garlic paste	: ½ tsp	Green coriander leaves	
Green chilli paste	: 1 tsp	(chopped)	: 2 tbsp
Tomato puree	: ½ cup	Water	: 3½ cups
Red chilli powder	: 2 tsp	Oil	: 7 tbsp
Turmeric powder	: 1 tsp	Salt as per taste	
Cumin powder (roasted)	: 1 tsp		

Procedure:

1) Make a mixture with tomato puree, yogurt, ginger garlic paste, green chilli paste, red chilli powder, turmeric powder, roasted cumin powder, garam masala powder, coriander powder and salt.

2) Take the chicken and marinate it in the same mixture. Let it rest for 3 to 4 hours.

3) Put oil in a pan, heat it and fry onions till they turn golden brown.

4) Now, to this add the marinated chicken and cook the entire mixture for 10 mins.

5) Next in a pressure cooker, take the rice and add 3½ cups of water to it. Also, take the saffron, mix with the milk and add to the rice.

6) Finally, add the cardamom powder and the chicken pieces, along with the marinade.

7) Mix all the ingredients gently, cover with the cooker lid and pressure cook for 1 whistle.

8) Garnish with green coriander leaves and serve hot.

Kozhikode Chicken Biryani
(Malabar style chicken Biryani)

Serves: 5

Cooking time (approx.): 40 minutes

Ingredients:

To marinate:

Chicken	: ½ kg	Cardamom	: 4–5
Yoghur	: ½ cup	Curry leaves	: 4–5
Coriander leaves		Cloves	: 4–5
(ground)	: 25 gm	Onion (chopped)	: 1
Mint leaves (ground)	: 25 gm	Broken rice	: 250 gm
Curry leaves	: 10 gm	Water	: ½ litre
Cumin seed powder	: ½ tsp	Salt	: 1 tsp
Coriander seed powder	: 1 tsp		
Aniseed powder (Saunf)	: ½ tsp	**To prepare the biryani masala:**	
Green chillies(chopped)	: 25 gm	Ghee	: 2 tbsp
Garlic	: 20 gm	Cinnamon	: 5–6 pieces
Ginger (chopped)	: 2 tsp	Bay leaf	: 1
Turmeric powder	: ½ tsp	Cloves	: 4–5
Lime juice	: 1 tsp	Cardamom seeds	: 4–5
Poppy seeds paste	: 1 tsp	Nutmeg	: 1
Salt as per taste		Onions	: 100 gms
		Tomato (medium sized, cut	
		into 4 pieces)	: 1
To prepare the rice:			
Ghee	: 1 tbsp	**For garnishing:**	
Cinnamon	: 5–6 pieces	Boiled egg	: 1
Bay leaf	: 1	Cashews and raisins (roasted in ghee)	

Procedure:

1) Make a mixture of yoghurt, ground coriander leaves, ground mint leaves, curry leaves, cumin seed powder, coriander seed powder, aniseed powder, green chillies,

garlic, ginger, turmeric powder, lime juice and poppy seed paste. Marinate the chicken pieces in this mixture and keep it aside for half an hour. Add salt.

2) *Put ghee in a pan and heat it.*

3) *Add to this cinnamon, bay leaf, cardamom seeds, curry leaves and cloves. Next, add onions and saute till they turn translucent.*

4) *Add the washed and drained rice to the above mixture along with the salt and cook till it turns translucent.*

5) *Add water to the rice and let it boil.*

6) *Once the water starts boiling, lower the flame and cover the vessel with a lid.*

7) *Cook the rice for the next 15 mins, over a low flame.*

8) *Put ghee in another pan and heat it.*

9) *Add to it, cinnamon, bay leaf, cardamom seeds, nutmeg and cloves.*

10) *Next, add onions and saute till they turn brown.*

11) *Then add the tomatoes and saute them too.*

12) *Now add the marinated chicken.*

13) *Cover the pan and cook over a medium flame for at least 5 mins.*

14) *Remove the lid and cook it for 10 mins more over a low flame. Allow the gravy to thicken.*

15) *Arrange the rice and the chicken masala in alternate layers in a serving bowl.*

16) *Garnish it by putting boiled egg (cut into 4 pieces), roasted cashews and raisins on the top layer.*

Ahmedi Biryani

Serves: 4

Cooking time (approx.): 75 minutes

Ingredients:

Chicken	: 500 gms	Green chilli (big)	: 1
Basmati rice (washed, soaked in water		Coriander leaves (chopped): ½ tbsp	
for 30 mins and drained)	: 1½ cups	Onion	: 1
Water	: 3 cups	Hot water	: ½ cup
Cinnamon	: 1" stick	Sugar	: 1 tsp
Bay leaf	: 1	Red chilli powder: ½ tsp	
Cloves	: 2	Coriander powder: ½ tsp	
Cardamoms	: 2	Fried cashew nuts and fried onion rings	
Black peppercorns	: 5	for garnishing	
Yoghurt	: 1 tbsp	Ghee: 1 tbsp	
Ginger-Garlic (chopped)	: 1 tbsp	Salt as per taste	

Procedure:

1) Pour 3 cups of water in a large pot.

2) Add to this, the rice, salt and half of all the spices.

3) Mix all these ingredients well. Cook the rice till it is half done.

4) Drain away the entire water, spread the rice on a plate and allow it to cool.

5) Take the onions and chop them into fine slices. Also, slit the green chillies.

6) Put ghee in another pan and heat it.

7) Wait till the ghee starts bubbling. Then add the remaining spices to it and saute till it gives out an aroma.

8) Next, take the chopped onions and add it to the pan. Saute till it turns golden brown in colour.

9) Add the chicken pieces, masala powders, green chilli, coriander leaves, ginger-garlic, salt and sugar.

10) Pour the hot water into it.

11) Mix it well. Cover it, simmer and cook for the next 20 mins or until the chicken pieces become soft.

12) Next, pour the yogurt. Simmer and wait till the gravy thickens.

13) Take another big pot and grease with melted ghee or butter.

14) Arrange the rice and the chicken in layers in the pot. Arrange them in alternate layers till the entire amount of rice and chicken has been used.

15) Cover the pot with a lid. Make dough from wheat flour and use it to seal the edges of the lid.

16) Place a tawa on the flame and put the sealed pot on the tava. This is done to ensure that the pot is not on the direct flame.

17) Cook the rice on a low flame for the next 25 mins or till the rice is fully cooked.

18) Alternately, the biryani can be baked in a preheated oven at 375°F or 185°C for 15–20 mins.

19) Garnish with fried cashew nuts and fried onion rings.

Afghani Biryani

Serves: 4–5
Cooking time (approx.): 35 minutes

Ingredients:

Whole chicken (cut into serving pieces)	: 1	Raisins for garnishing	
		Whole cardamom seeds	: 10
Basmati rice (washed and pre-soaked)	: 2 cups	Cloves (long)	: 10
		Cinnamon stick	: 1" piece
Onion (peeled and chopped)	: 1	Cumin seeds	: ½ tsp
		Water	: 6 cups
Carrot (chopped)	: 1	Salt as per taste	
Tomatoes (pureed in blender)	: 7	Black pepper powder as per requirement	
Almonds (slivered and fried) for garnishing		Cooking oil as per requirement	

Procedure:

1) Take the carrots and onions and sauté in the cooking oil.

2) Add to this the chicken and mix well.

3) Next, add cardamom seeds, cloves, cinnamon stick, cumin seeds, salt and pepper powder. Mix well.

4) The chicken should be half-cooked.

5) Add the tomato puree to the half-done chicken and mix. Cover the pot and cook over a low flame until the chicken is well-cooked.

6) Put the rice in a separate pot and boil it in water. When cooked, drain the water.

7) As the final step, cover the rice with the chicken and the spices, cover the pot and cook it over a very low flame for the next 5 mins.

8) In order to add to the exquisite taste, garnish it with fried almonds and raisins.

Eggs Biryani

Serves: 3–4

Cooking time (approx.): 35 minutes

Ingredients:

Basmati rice (washed and soaked for 30 mins)	: 2 cups	Ginger-garlic paste	: 2 tbsp
		Onion	: 1
		Cinnamon	: 2 sticks
Water	: 3½ cups	Cloves	: 3
Oil	: 6–8 tbsp	Coriander leaves (chopped)	: A few
Eggs (boiled)	: 4	Turmeric powder	: ¼ tsp
Green chillies	: 5	Salt as per taste	

Procedure:

1) Cut each egg into 2 halves to make 8 egg halves. Also chop the chillies and onions into small pieces.

2) Put some oil in a pan, heat it and then add cinnamon, cloves, ginger-garlic paste, chillies and onions. Fry for 3 mins.

3) Add rice to the pan along with the water, eggs, turmeric powder and salt.

4) Cook on high flame till the water reaches boiling point and then cover with lid and simmer on low heat till done.

5) Garnish with coriander leaves and serve hot.

Prawn Biryani

Serves: 2

Cooking time (approx.): 20 minutes

Ingredients:

Prawns	: 20	Coriander seeds	: 1 tsp
Basmati rice (washed,		Aniseeds	: 1 tsp
soaked in water for		Cinnamon stick (small)	: 1
30 mins and drained)	: 1 cup	Cloves	: 3
Water	: 1½ cups	Kesari or saffron powder	: A pinch
Onion(thinly chopped)	: 1 cup	Mint leaves (leaves)	: ¼ cup
Tomato(finely chopped)	: ¾ cup	Coriander leaves (finely	
Ginger	: 2" piece	chopped)	: 4 tbsp
Garlic	: 8 cloves	Oil	: 3 tsp
Green chilli	: 1	Ghee or dalda	: 2 tsp
Turmeric powder	: ¾ tsp	Mitha attar	: 3–4 drops
Red chilli powder	: 1 tsp	Salt as per taste	

Procedure:

1) Clean the prawns.

2) Make a fine paste by grinding ginger, garlic and aniseeds.

3) Heat oil in a pressure cooker and put cinnamon stick and cloves into it. Fry for a few seconds.

4) Next, add ginger-garlic–aniseed paste, mint leaves, coriander leaves, onion and tomato. Fry well.

5) Add the prawn to the above masala and fry for a minute.

6) Add turmeric powder, chilli powder, 1½ cups of water, salt, rice and mitha attar. Stir well.

7) Cover the cooker with the lid. Remove the weight. Next, turn the flame to medium high.

8) Once the steam starts coming out from the nozzle, the weight should be put on the cooker. Next, turn the flame to medium low. Keep it in that position for 8 minutes.

9) Remove the pressure cooker from the flame and keep it aside.

10) Open the lid after 10 mins, mix the rice well and serve with onion raita.

Shrimp Biryani

Cooking time (approx.): 50 minutes

Ingredients:

Shrimp (shelled and deveined)	: 500 gms	Coconut (grated)	: 1 cup
Peas	: A handful	Garam masala powder	: 2 tsp
Basmati rice	: 2 cups	Lime juice	: 1 tbsp
Onion (medium sized, chopped)	: 2	Cashew nuts and raisins	: 1 tbsp
		Bay leaves	: 2
Ginger (grated)	: 1" piece	Water	: 4 cups
Garlic (crushed)	: 4 cloves	Ghee or butter	: 6 tbsp
Green chillies	: 3	Salt as per taste	

Procedure:

1) Wash the rice and soak it in plain water for 10 minutes.

2) Make a paste with the green chillies, garam masala powder, ginger, garlic and coconut.

3) Put 3 tbsp of ghee or butter in a pan and heat it. Add to this half of the onion and fry it till it becomes golden brown in colour.

4) Add the ground masala paste and salt to the onion and stir it for the next 5 minutes.

5) Add the shrimps and salt.

6) Mix the shrimp well so that it is well coated with the masala. Cook it over a low flame for the next 5 minutes. When done, remove it from flame and keep aside.

7) Take another pan and heat 3 tbsp of butter or ghee in it. Put the bay leaves into it and fry. Next, put the remaining onions into it and fry till it turns golden brown in color.

8) *Add the rice and for the next 10 minutes stir fry it. Next, add the peas and 4 cups of water.*

9) *Cover the pan with the lid. Let the rice cook for the next 15 minutes over a low flame.*

10) *Preheat the oven at 300°F or 150°C.*

11) *Mix the shrimps and the rice in a greased serving bowl.*

12) *Take an aluminum foil and cover the top of the pan with it. Put the pan in the oven and bake for 10 to 15 minutes.*

13) *Once done, add lime juice to the rice. Garnish it with fried cashew nuts and raisins.*

Mutton Biryani

Ingredients: ─────────────────────────────

Rice (preferably not very fine basmati, washed, soaked in water for 30 mins and drained)	: 750 gms	Cinnamon sticks (1"pieces)	: 1–2
		Cloves	: A few
Mutton (make sure that the mutton is cut of leg, chops and certain no. of boneless pieces)	: 1 kg	Green cardamom	: 7–8
		Whole black peppercorns	: 6–7
		Cumin seeds	: 1 tsp
Yoghurt	: 75 gms	Bay leaves	: 8–12
Onions	: 4–5	Salt as per taste	
Garlic (medium sized)	: A handful	Ground pepper powder	: A little

Procedure:

1) Wash the mutton pieces thoroughly and drain away the water. Put the mutton in a bowl and put into it yogurt, half of the whole garam masala and 3 to 4 bay leaves. Mix the ingredients well so that each piece is coated. Add salt and pepper powder to this. Refrigerate. Leave it for at least 4 to 5 hours. For best results, keep overnight.

2) Measure the quantity of rice being used, with a hollow utensil. Note amount. Wash the rice thoroughly with water and soak the rice in sufficient amount of water for half an hour.

3) Slice the onions.

4) Take the garlic cloves and peel them. Slice them into two pieces lengthwise.

5) Heat a little oil in a pan and add half the sliced onions. Fry till the onions change colour into golden brown. Once they are fried, place the onions on a paper towel so that the excess oil is soaked.

6) Take the balance whole spices and bay leaves and put them into the oil that is left after

frying the onions. Cook these over a low flame for a few seconds. Wait till the spices begin changing their colors and then add all of the garlic cloves. Cook this for a few seconds before adding the remaining onion. Let the onions glaze over a low flame. Add salt according to your taste.

7) Take each of the mutton pieces and squeeze it gently in order to remove the excess marinade. Add the mutton pieces, one by one, to the oil.

8) Now, for the next 15 to 20 min, fry or cook the mutton pieces. Then add the yogurt marinade to it and cook it further for the next 15 mins.

9) Put the mutton in a pressure cooker and cook it in full steam for 10 to 12 mins. After this, cook it over a low heat for another 15 mins.

10) When it is done, remove the pressure cooker from the fire. Let all the steam escape from it and then open the lid. Pass the contents through a strainer. Keep aside the mutton pieces.

11) Mash the onion/garlic and the whole spices mixture left in the strainer, with the help of a ladle. Add it to the liquid. Now take the same bowl that was used to measure the rice and use it to measure the amount of liquid. This liquid should be exactly double the amount of rice used. If, in any case, the liquid falls short of the required amount, then add some lukewarm water to it.

12) Now grease the inner wall of a heavy-bottomed pan with oil or butter. Take the bay leaves and make a layer with it in such a way that the entire surface of the pan is covered.

13) Make a layer with the uncooked rice. Top this layer with a layer of mutton pieces. Then take the liquid and add a few ladlefuls to it. Make sure to turn the pan while adding the liquid. This will help in spreading it evenly.

14) Repeat this process again, beginning with rice and ending with the liquid spread. Continue doing this till all the mutton, rice and the liquid is used up. Also, note that the last layer should be that of rice.

15) Take the fried onions and add the pieces in between the layers. Spread some on the top layer as well.

16) *Take dough and roll it into a cylindrical shape. Cover the pan with a lid that's exactly the same size as its mouth and seal it firmly by wrapping the dough around the rim of the pan and lid. Place this pan on a fire and place some weight on the lid. Put it on a high fire and cook it for the first 5 to 6 mins. Next, turn the fire low and cook it for say another 12 to 15 mins.*

17) *When the dough becomes hard and crispy, it means that the biryani is done. Now remove it from the fire and serve hot.*

Nawabi Biryani

Serves: 6–8

Cooking time (approx.): 60 minutes

Ingredients:

Basmati rice (washed , soaked in water for 30 mins and drained) : 3½ cups		Shah jeera (black cumin seeds)	: ½ tsp
Mutton (cut in pieces)	: ½ kg	Turmeric powder	: ½ tsp
Onions (sliced)	: 3	Saffron (dissolved in ¼ cup warm milk)	: 1 pinch
Ginger-Garlic paste	: ½ tbsp		
Garam masala powder	: 1 tsp	Jardalu (Apricots)	: 5
Red chillies	: 3	Water	: 6½ cups
Cinnamon stick	: 1" piece	Dry fruits as required	
Curd (beaten)	: ½ cup	Coriander leaves and pudina (mint) leaves as required	
Green cardamom	: 3		
Peppercorns	: 5	Ghee as per requirement	
Cloves	: 5		

Procedure:

1) Take 2 ½ tbsp of ghee. Put some salt in it and fry the dry fruits and apricots. Make a fine paste by grinding red chillies and fried onion.

2) Make a mixture of curd, ginger-garlic paste, onion-chilli paste, turmeric powder and salt and marinate the mutton pieces in it. Put some ghee in a pressure cooker heat it, and then add the marinated mutton into it. Pressure cook it until done.

3) Put some ghee in another vessel and heat it. Add to this the whole spices and fry them for a while. Now add the rice. Add some salt and warm water. Cook the rice till all the water has been absorbed.

4) Once the rice is cooked, spread it out and let it cool. Also, remove the whole spices

that were added to it. Grease the inner wall of a heavy-bottomed pan with ghee. Put the cooked mutton into it and sprinkle some garam masala powder.

5) *Follow this with a layer of rice, then melted ghee and then saffron milk. Add to this the fried nuts and cover it with a tight fitting lid. For the next 15 to 20 mins, keep it on dum on low flame.*

6) *Mix it well and serve hot. Garnish the dish with chopped coriander and pudina leaves.*

Badshahi Biryani

Serves: 6–8

Cooking time (approx.): 75 minutes

Ingredients:

Mutton	: ½ kg	Oil	: 1 tbsp
Rice (parboiled)	: 250 gms	Garlic	: 4 pods
Lemon juice	: 1½ tbsp	Cloves	: 2
Almonds (blanched)	: 10	Ginger	: 1 " long piece
Mint Leaves (Pudina leaves)	: ½ tbsp	Saffron	: ½ tbsp
Butter	: 1 cups	Green chilli (chopped)	: ½ tbsp
Coriander leaves (chopped)	: A handful	Red chilli powder	: ½ tbsp
Cumin seeds	: ½ tbsp	Cinnamon	: ½"
Onion (large sized)	: 2	Curd	: ½ kg
Brown cardamom	: 2	Milk	: 125 gms
		Water	: 3 cups

Procedure:

1) Begin with the rice. Wash it well and then soak it.

2) Take the sliced onions and fry them till they turn golden brown in color.

3) Put some water in the saffron and let it soak.

4) Take ginger, red chilies, garlic and almonds and grind them together. Add this to some butter and fry.

5) Next, take the above fried masala and add it to the mutton and salt stir the whole thing for the next 5 mins.

6) Add water to the mutton and cook till the mutton becomes soft. Also note that about 1 cup of gravy should be left behind.

7) Put rice in another pan. Add salt to it and let it boil.

8) Take the curd and place it on a piece of muslin cloth. Wait for a while and allow the water to drain away. Next, add to this, cloves, cardamoms, cumin seed, mint leaves, chopped chillies and coriander.

9) Also, drain away the water from the saffron and add lemon juice to it.

10) Put the above ingredients in the mutton.

11) Take half of the boiled rice and spread it over the mutton as a layer. Follow this with a layer of fried onions and then of rice again.

12) Pour some milk and butter into it and cover the vessel.

13) Take some flour paste and use it to seal the edges of the vessel.

14) Place the vessel on the flame for an hour.

15) When done, team it with curry and serve hot.

Shahjahani Biryani

It is a Mughal dish and is traditionally served with baingan bharta (spicy brinjal).

Serves: 4–5

Cooking time (approx.): 50 minutes

Ingredients:

Mutton	: ½ kg	Garlic	: 4 pods
Rice (parboiled)	: 250 gms	Cloves	: 2
Lemon juice	: 1½ tbsp	Ginger	: 1" long
Almonds (blanched)	: 10		piece
Mint leaves	: ½ tbsp	Saffron	: ½ tbsp
Butter	: 1 cup	Green chillies (finely	
Coriander leaves		chopped)	: ½ tbsp
(chopped)	: A handful	Red chilli powder	: ½ tbsp
Cumin seeds	: ½ tbsp	Cinnamon	: ½"
Onion (large sized,		Curd (hung curd)	: ½ kg
sliced)	: 2	Milk	: 1cup
Brown cardamom	: 2	Water	: 3 cups
Oil	: 1 tbsp		

Procedure:

1) Begin with the rice. Wash it well and then soak it.

2) Take the sliced onions and fry them till they turn golden brown in color.

3) Put some water in the saffron and let it soak.

4) Take ginger, red chilies, garlic and almonds and grind them together. Add this to some butter and fry.

5) Next, take the above fried masala and add it to the mutton and salt stir the whole thing for the next 5 mins.

6) Add water to the mutton and cook till the mutton becomes soft. Also note that about 1 cup of gravy should be left behind.

7) *Put rice in another pan. Add salt to it and let it boil.*

8) *Take the curd and place it on a piece of muslin cloth. Wait for a while and allow the water to drain away. Next, add to this, cloves, cardamoms, cumin seed, mint leaves, chopped chillies and coriander.*

9) *Also, drain away the water from the saffron and add lemon juice to it.*

10) *Put the above ingredients in the mutton.*

11) *Take half of the boiled rice and spread it over the mutton as a layer. Follow this with a layer of fried onions and then of rice again.*

12) *Pour some milk and butter into it and cover the vessel.*

13) *Take some flour paste and use it to seal the edges of the vessel.*

14) *Place the vessel on the flame for an hour.*

To serve: *Serve it hot. You can also team it up with some curry that you have prepared from beforehand.*

Notes

Notes